Life Lessons

from THE INSPIRED WORD of GOD

BOOK of LUKE

MAX LUCADO

General Editor

LIFE LESSONS FROM THE INSPIRED WORD OF GOD—BOOK OF LUKE

Scripture passages taken from:

 The Holy Bible, *New Century Version* (NCV)
Copyright ©1987, 1988, 1991 by Word Publishing. All rights reserved.

 The Holy Bible, *New King James Version* (NKJV)
Copyright © 1979, 1980, 1982 by Thomas Nelson. All rights reserved.

All excerpts used by permission.

Design and cover art—by Koechel Peterson and Associates, Inc., Minneapolis, Minnesota.

Produced with the assistance of the Livingstone Corporation.

ISBN: 0-8499-5325-1
Published by Word Publishing

TABLE OF CONTENTS

HOW TO STUDY THE BIBLE

BY MAX LUCADO

*T*his is a peculiar book you are holding. Words crafted in another language. Deeds done in a distant era. Events recorded in a far-off land. Counsel offered to a foreign people. This is a peculiar book.

It's surprising that anyone reads it. It's too old. Some of its writings date back five thousand years. It's too bizarre. The book speaks of incredible floods, fires, earthquakes, and people with supernatural abilities. It's too radical. The Bible calls for undying devotion to a carpenter who called himself God's Son.

Logic says this book shouldn't survive. Too old, too bizarre, too radical.

The Bible has been banned, burned, scoffed, and ridiculed. Scholars have mocked it as foolish. Kings have branded it as illegal. A thousand times over it the grave has been dug and the dirge has begun, but somehow the Bible never stays in the grave. Not only has it survived, it has thrived. It is the single most popular book in all of history. It has been the best-selling book in the world for years!

There is no way on earth to explain it. Which perhaps is the only explanation. The answer? The Bible's durability is not found on earth; it is found in heaven. For the millions who have tested its claims and claimed its promises, there is but one answer—the Bible is God's book and God's voice.

As you read it, you would be wise to give some thought to two questions. What is the purpose of the Bible? and How do I study the Bible? Time spent reflecting on these two issues will greatly enhance your Bible study.

What is the purpose of the Bible?

Let the Bible itself answer that question.

Since you were a child you have known the Holy Scriptures which are able to make you wise. And that wisdom leads to salvation through faith in Christ Jesus.

(2 Tim. 3:15)

The purpose of the Bible? Salvation. God's highest passion is to get his children home. His book, the Bible, describes his plan of salvation. The purpose of the Bible is to proclaim God's plan and passion to save his children.

That is the reason this book has endured through the centuries. It dares to tackle the toughest questions about life: Where do I go after I die? Is there a God? What do I do with my fears? The Bible offers answers to these crucial questions. It is the treasure map that leads us to God's highest treasure, eternal life.

But how do we use the Bible? Countless copies of Scripture sit unread on bookshelves and nightstands simply because people don't know how to read it. What can we do to make the Bible real in our lives?

The clearest answer is found in the words of Jesus.

"Ask," he promised, *"and God will give to you. Search, and you will find. Knock, and the door will open for you."*

(Matt. 7:7)

The first step in understanding the Bible is asking God to help us. We should read prayerfully. If anyone understands God's Word, it is because of God and not the reader.

But the Helper will teach you everything and will cause you to remember all that I told you. The Helper is the Holy Spirit whom the Father will send in my name.

(John 14:26)

Before reading the Bible, pray. Invite God to speak to you. Don't go to Scripture looking for your idea, go searching for his.

Not only should we read the Bible prayerfully, we should read it carefully. *Search and you will find* is the pledge. The Bible is not a newspaper to be skimmed but rather a mine to be quarried. *Search for it like silver, and hunt for it like hidden treasure. Then you will understand respect for the LORD, and you will find that you know God* (Prov. 2:4).

Any worthy find requires effort. The Bible is no exception. To understand the Bible you don't have to be brilliant, but you must be willing to roll up your sleeves and search.

Be a worker who is not ashamed and who uses the true teaching in the right way.

(2 Tim. 2:15)

Here's a practical point. Study the Bible a bit at a time. Hunger is not satisfied by eating twenty-one meals in one sitting once a week. The body needs a steady diet to remain strong. So does the soul. When God sent food to his people in the wilderness, he didn't provide loaves already made. Instead, he sent them manna in the shape of *thin flakes like frost . . . on the desert ground* (Exod. 16:14).

God gave manna in limited portions.

God sends spiritual food the same way. He opens the heavens with just enough nutrients for today's hunger. He provides, *a command here, a command there. A rule here, a rule there. A little lesson here, a little lesson there* (Isa. 28:10).

Don't be discouraged if your reading reaps a small harvest. Some days a lesser portion is all that is needed. What is important is to search every day for that day's message. A steady diet of God's Word over a lifetime builds a healthy soul and mind.

A little girl returned from her first day at school. Her mom asked, "Did you learn anything?" "Apparently not enough," the girl responded, "I have to go back tomorrow and the next day and the next. . . ."

Such is the case with learning. And such is the case with Bible study. Understanding comes little by little over a lifetime.

There is a third step in understanding the Bible. After the asking and seeking comes the knocking. After you ask and search, then knock.

Knock, and the door will open for you.
(Matt. 7:7)

To knock is to stand at God's door. To make yourself available. To climb the steps, cross the porch, stand at the doorway, and volunteer. Knocking goes beyond the realm of thinking and into the realm of acting.

To knock is to ask, What can I do? How can I obey? Where can I go?

It's one thing to know what to do. It's another to do it. But for those who do it, those who choose to obey, a special reward awaits them.

The truly happy are those who carefully study God's perfect law that makes people free, and they continue to study it. They do not forget what they heard, but they obey what God's teaching says. Those who do this will be made happy.

(James 1:25)

What a promise. Happiness comes to those who do what they read! It's the same with medicine. If you only read the label but ignore the pills, it won't help. It's the same with food. If you only read the recipe but never cook, you won't be fed. And it's the same with the Bible. If you only read the words but never obey, you'll never know the joy God has promised.

Ask. Search. Knock. Simple, isn't it? Why don't you give it a try? If you do, you'll see why you are holding the most remarkable book in history.

LUKE

INTRODUCTION

Nearly two thousand years ago a doctor named Luke began a letter to a friend with these words:

Many have tried to report on the things that happened among us. They have written the same things that we learned from others— the people who saw those things from the beginning and served God by telling people his message. Since I myself have studied everything carefully from the beginning, most excellent Theophilus, it seemed good for me to write it out for you. I arranged it in order to help you know that what you have been taught is true (1:1–4).

Luke and Theophilus shared two loves. A love for Christ and a love for the facts. They didn't want legends, they wanted truth. And so Dr. Luke begins to sort the truth and report the facts to Theophilus. The result is part letter and part research paper.

It is part letter because it was written for a friend. What a bond must have existed between these two that Luke would labor so! It is part research paper, because Luke had *studied everything carefully from the beginning* and he wanted Theophilus to benefit from his study.

Can't you envision him in the home of Mary, "Tell me again what happened in Bethlehem." Can't you see him peppering Matthew with questions? "Let me see if I got this parable right." Or on long walks with Peter, "When you denied him the third time, did Jesus know?"

With the skill of a surgeon, Luke probes for truth. Why? So his friend could know that what he had been taught was true.

Did Luke have any idea that millions of us would benefit from his study? I doubt it. All he did was share the truth with a friend.

Can you imagine what would happen if we all did the same?

LESSON ONE

HOPE IN GOD

REFLECTION

Begin your study by sharing thoughts on this question.

1. Think of a time when God did an amazing work in a friend's life. What hope did that give you?

_____

_____

_____

BIBLE READING

Read Luke 1:5–25 from the NCV or the NKJV.

NCV

⁵During the time Herod ruled Judea, there was a priest named Zechariah who belonged to Abijah's group. Zechariah's wife, Elizabeth, came from the family of Aaron. ⁶Zechariah and Elizabeth truly did what God said was good. They did everything the Lord commanded and were without fault in keeping his law. ⁷But they had no children, because Elizabeth could not have a baby, and both of them were very old.

⁸One day Zechariah was serving as a priest before God, because his group was on duty.

NKJV

⁵There was in the days of Herod, the king of Judea, a certain priest named Zacharias, of the division of Abijah. His wife *was* of the daughters of Aaron, and her name *was* Elizabeth. ⁶And they were both righteous before God, walking in all the commandments and ordinances of the Lord blameless. ⁷But they had no child, because Elizabeth was barren, and they were both well advanced in years.

⁸So it was, that while he was serving as priest before God in the order of his division,

NCV

⁹According to the custom of the priests, he was chosen by lot to go into the Temple of the Lord and burn incense. ¹⁰There were a great many people outside praying at the time the incense was offered. ¹¹Then an angel of the Lord appeared to Zechariah, standing on the right side of the incense table. ¹²When he saw the angel, Zechariah was startled and frightened. ¹³But the angel said to him, "Zechariah, don't be afraid. God has heard your prayer. Your wife, Elizabeth, will give birth to a son, and you will name him John. ¹⁴He will bring you joy and gladness, and many people will be happy because of his birth. ¹⁵John will be a great man for the Lord. He will never drink wine or beer, and even from birth, he will be filled with the Holy Spirit. ¹⁶He will help many people of Israel return to the Lord their God. ¹⁷He will go before the Lord in spirit and power like Elijah. He will make peace between parents and their children and will bring those who are not obeying God back to the right way of thinking, to make a people ready for the coming of the Lord."

¹⁸Zechariah said to the angel, "How can I know that what you say is true? I am an old man, and my wife is old, too."

¹⁹The angel answered him, "I am Gabriel. I stand before God, who sent me to talk to you and to tell you this good news. ²⁰Now, listen! You will not be able to speak until the day these things happen, because you did not believe what I told you. But they will really happen."

²¹Outside, the people were still waiting for Zechariah and were surprised that he was staying so long in the Temple. ²²When Zechariah came outside, he could not speak to them, and

NKJV

⁹according to the custom of the priesthood, his lot fell to burn incense when he went into the temple of the Lord. ¹⁰And the whole multitude of the people was praying outside at the hour of incense. ¹¹Then an angel of the Lord appeared to him, standing on the right side of the altar of incense. ¹²And when Zacharias saw *him,* he was troubled, and fear fell upon him.

¹³But the angel said to him, "Do not be afraid, Zacharias, for your prayer is heard; and your wife Elizabeth will bear you a son, and you shall call his name John. ¹⁴And you will have joy and gladness, and many will rejoice at his birth. ¹⁵For he will be great in the sight of the Lord, and shall drink neither wine nor strong drink. He will also be filled with the Holy Spirit, even from his mother's womb. ¹⁶And he will turn many of the children of Israel to the Lord their God. ¹⁷He will also go before Him in the spirit and power of Elijah, 'to turn the hearts of the fathers to the children,' and the disobedient to the wisdom of the just, to make ready a people prepared for the Lord."

¹⁸And Zacharias said to the angel, "How shall I know this? For I am an old man, and my wife is well advanced in years."

¹⁹And the angel answered and said to him, "I am Gabriel, who stands in the presence of God, and was sent to speak to you and bring you these glad tidings. ²⁰But behold, you will be mute and not able to speak until the day these things take place, because you did not believe my words which will be fulfilled in their own time."

²¹And the people waited for Zacharias, and marveled that he lingered so long in the

NCV

they knew he had seen a vision in the Temple. He could only make signs to them and remained unable to speak. ²³When his time of service at the Temple was finished, he went home.

²⁴Later, Zechariah's wife, Elizabeth, became pregnant and did not go out of her house for five months. Elizabeth said, ²⁵"Look what the Lord has done for me! My people were ashamed of me, but now the Lord has taken away that shame."

NKJV

temple. ²²But when he came out, he could not speak to them; and they perceived that he had seen a vision in the temple, for he beckoned to them and remained speechless.

²³And so it was, as soon as the days of his service were completed, that he departed to his own house. ²⁴Now after those days his wife Elizabeth conceived; and she hid herself five months, saying, ²⁵"Thus the Lord has dealt with me, in the days when He looked on me, to take away my reproach among people."

DISCOVERY

Explore the Bible reading by discussing these questions.

2. What kind of reputation did Zechariah and Elizabeth have in their community?

_____

_____

_____

3. How did Zechariah and Elizabeth cope with the humiliation of childlessness?

_____

_____

_____

4. The angel promised a child. In what way did this offer hope to Zechariah in his situation?

_____

_____

_____

5. Why did Zechariah doubt God's promise?

_____

_____

_____

6. In what way did Elizabeth react to the fulfillment of the angel's prophecy?

_____

_____

_____

INSPIRATION

Here is an uplifting thought from *The Inspirational Bible*.

Hope is not what you expect; it is what you would never dream. It is a wild, improbable tale with a pinch-me-I'm-dreaming ending. It's Abraham adjusting his bifocals so he can see not his grandson, but his son. It's Moses standing in the Promised Land not with Aaron or Miriam at his side, but with Elijah and the transfigured Christ. It's Zechariah left speechless at the sight of wife Elizabeth, gray-headed and pregnant. And it is the two Emmaus-bound pilgrims reaching out to take a piece of bread only to see the hands from which it is offered are pierced.

Hope is not a granted wish or a favor performed; no, it is far greater than that. It is a zany, unpredictable dependence on a God who loves to surprise us out of our socks and be there in the flesh to see our reaction.

(From *God Came Near*
by Max Lucado)

RESPONSE

Use these questions to share more deeply with each other.

7. Why do we sometimes doubt God's desire to fulfill our deepest longings?

_____

_____

_____

8. What comfort or encouragement does this passage offer to us when we find ourselves in seemingly hopeless situations?

_____

_____

_____

9. What steps can we take to deal with feelings of hopelessness?

_____

_____

_____

PRAYER

Thank you, Father, for giving us hope in a world of broken promises and dashed dreams. You have proven your trustworthiness by keeping your promises to your people. O Father, you are our only hope. Strengthen our dependence on you, give us patience to wait for your perfect timing, and teach us to rejoice in your goodness.

JOURNALING

Take a few moments to record your personal insights from this lesson.

What personal hopes or dreams am I tempted to give up? How can I entrust them to God?

ADDITIONAL QUESTIONS

10. In what way does this passage affect your attitude toward your frustrations and problems?

_____

_____

_____

11. What is keeping you from expecting God to do spectacular things in your life?

_____

_____

_____

12. In what way can you demonstrate your faith in God's promises?

_____

_____

_____

For more Bible passages on hope, see Psalm 42:5; 62:5; 130:7; Proverbs 23:18; Jeremiah 29:11; Lamentations 3:21–24; Romans 12:12; 15:4; 1 Timothy 4:9–10; 6:17; Titus 1:1–2.

To complete the Book of Luke during this twelve-part study, read Luke 1:1—3:38.

LESSON TWO

FAITH AT WORK

REFLECTION

Begin your study by sharing thoughts on this question.

1. Think of a time when you have seen faith at work. What were the results of that faith?

_____

_____

_____

BIBLE READING

Read Luke 5:17–26 from the NCV or the NKJV.

NCV

¹⁷One day as Jesus was teaching the people, the Pharisees and teachers of the law from every town in Galilee and Judea and from Jerusalem were there. The Lord was giving Jesus the power to heal people. ¹⁸Just then, some men were carrying on a mat a man who was paralyzed. They tried to bring him in and put him down before Jesus. ¹⁹But because there were so many people there, they could not find a way in. So they went up on the roof and lowered the man on his mat through the ceiling

NKJV

¹⁷Now it happened on a certain day, as He was teaching, that there were Pharisees and teachers of the law sitting by, who had come out of every town of Galilee, Judea, and Jerusalem. And the power of the Lord was *present* to heal them. ¹⁸Then behold, men brought on a bed a man who was paralyzed, whom they sought to bring in and lay before Him. ¹⁹And when they could not find how they might bring him in, because of the crowd, they went up on the housetop and let him down with *his* bed

NCV	NKJV
into the middle of the crowd right before Jesus. ²⁰Seeing their faith, Jesus said, "Friend, your sins are forgiven."	through the tiling into the midst before Jesus. ²⁰When He saw their faith, He said to him, "Man, your sins are forgiven you."
²¹The Jewish teachers of the law and the Pharisees thought to themselves, "Who is this man who is speaking as if he were God? Only God can forgive sins."	²¹And the scribes and the Pharisees began to reason, saying, "Who is this who speaks blasphemies? Who can forgive sins but God alone?"
²²But Jesus knew what they were thinking and said, "Why are you thinking these things? ²³Which is easier: to say, 'Your sins are forgiven,' or to say, 'Stand up and walk'?²⁴But I will prove to you that the Son of Man has authority on earth to forgive sins." So Jesus said to the paralyzed man, "I tell you, stand up, take your mat, and go home."	²²But when Jesus perceived their thoughts, He answered and said to them, "Why are you reasoning in your hearts? ²³Which is easier, to say, 'Your sins are forgiven you,' or to say, 'Rise up and walk'? ²⁴But that you may know that the Son of Man has power on earth to forgive sins"—He said to the man who was paralyzed, "I say to you, arise, take up your bed, and go to your house."
²⁵At once the man stood up before them, picked up his mat, and went home, praising God. ²⁶All the people were fully amazed and began to praise God. They were filled with much respect and said, "Today we have seen amazing things!"	²⁵Immediately he rose up before them, took up what he had been lying on, and departed to his own house, glorifying God. ²⁶And they were all amazed, and they glorified God and were filled with fear, saying, "We have seen strange things today!"

DISCOVERY

Explore the Bible reading by discussing these questions.

2. This group of men brought their paralyzed friend to Jesus. What do you think they thought Jesus would do for him?

_____

_____

_____

3. What risks and obstacles did the men face because of the crowd around Jesus?

_____

_____

_____

4. What were the pros and cons of their plan to let their friend down through the roof?

_____

_____

_____

5. What did the fact that these men would do anything to get their friend to Jesus reveal about their view of Jesus?

_____

_____

_____

6. Why was Jesus' first response to forgive rather than to heal?

_____

_____

_____

INSPIRATION

Here is an uplifting thought from *The Inspirational Bible.*

Whether he was born paralyzed or became paralyzed—the end result was the same: total dependence on others. . . . When people looked at him, they didn't see the man; they saw a body in need of a miracle. That's not what Jesus saw, but that's what the people saw. And that's certainly what his friends saw. So they did what any of us would do for a friend. They tried to get him some help. . . .

By the time his friends arrived at the place, the house was full. People jammed the doorways. Kids sat in the windows. Others peeked over shoulders. How would this small band of friends ever attract Jesus' attention? They had to make a choice. Do we go in or give up?

What would have happened had the friends given up? What if they had shrugged their shoulders and mumbled something about the crowd being big and dinner getting cold and turned and left? After all, they had done a good deed in coming this far. Who could fault them for turning back? You can only do so much for somebody. But these friends hadn't done enough.

One said that he had an idea. The four huddled over the paralytic and listened to the plan to climb to the top of the house, cut through the roof, and lower their friend down with their sashes.

It was risky—they could fall. It was dangerous—*he* could fall. It was unorthodox—de-roofing is antisocial. It was intrusive—Jesus was busy. But it was their only chance to see Jesus. So they climbed to the roof.

Faith does these things. Faith does the unexpected. And faith gets God's attention. . . .

Jesus was moved by the scene of faith. So he applauds—if not with his hands, at least with his heart. And not only does he applaud, he blesses. And we witness a divine loveburst.

The friends want him to heal their friend. But Jesus won't settle for a simple healing of the body—he wants to heal the soul. He leapfrogs the physical and deals with the spiritual. To heal the body is temporal; to heal the soul is eternal. . . . So strong was his love for this crew of faith that he went beyond their appeal and went straight to the cross.

Jesus already knows the cost of grace. He already knows the price of forgiveness. But he offers it anyway. Love bursts in his heart. . . .

And though we can't hear it here, the angels can hear him there. All of heaven must pause as another burst of love declares the only words that really matter: "Your sins are forgiven."

(From *He Still Moves Stones* by Max Lucado)

RESPONSE

Use these questions to share more deeply with each other.

7. In what way did the four friends' faith in Jesus affect the life of the paralyzed man?

_____

_____

_____

8. In what ways does your faith affect others around you?

_____

_____

_____

9. List some practical ways we can show our faith in Jesus Christ.

_____

_____

_____

PRAYER

Father, when all the doors are closed, give us the courage to persevere. When no solutions are in sight, help us to find new ways to break through the barriers that separate us from you. May we persistently seek your face and daily demonstrate our faith in you.

JOURNALING

Take a few moments to record your personal insights from this lesson.

What step of faith am I willing to take this week to be closer to God?

ADDITIONAL QUESTIONS

10. What risks or obstacles have you faced in living out your beliefs?

_____

_____

_____

11. In what way have those difficulties stretched and strengthened your faith?

_____

_____

_____

12. In what way have you seen God bless people who trust him?

_____

_____

_____

For more Bible passages on faith, see 2 Chronicles 20:20; Matthew 9:2; Mark 11:22; Luke 7:9; John 8:30; Acts 3:16; Romans 4:16–25; 1 Corinthians 2:5; 16:13; 2 Corinthians 5:7; Galatians 2:16; Philippians 3:8–9; 1 Timothy 6:11–12; Hebrews 11:1–40; James 2:14–26.

To complete the Book of Luke during this twelve-part study, read Luke 4:1–5:39.

ADDITIONAL THOUGHTS

LESSON THREE

PRAYER THAT STRENGTHENS

REFLECTION

Begin your study by sharing thoughts on this question.

1. Describe a time when you felt strengthened through prayer.

_____

_____

_____

BIBLE READING

Read Luke 6:1–16 from the NCV or the NKJV.

NCV

¹One Sabbath day Jesus was walking through some fields of grain. His followers picked the heads of grain, rubbed them in their hands, and ate them. ²Some Pharisees said, "Why do you do what is not lawful on the Sabbath day?"

³Jesus answered, "Have you not read what David did when he and those with him were hungry? ⁴He went into God's house and took and ate the holy bread, which is lawful only for priests to eat. And he gave some to the people who were with him." ⁵Then Jesus said to the

NKJV

¹Now it happened on the second Sabbath after the first that He went through the grainfields. And His disciples plucked the heads of grain and ate *them*, rubbing *them* in *their* hands. ²And some of the Pharisees said to them, "Why are you doing what is not lawful to do on the Sabbath?"

³But Jesus answering them said, "Have you not even read this, what David did when he was hungry, he and those who were with him: ⁴how he went into the house of God, took and ate the showbread, and also gave some to those with

NCV

Pharisees, "The Son of Man is Lord of the Sabbath day."

⁶On another Sabbath day Jesus went into the synagogue and was teaching, and a man with a crippled right hand was there. ⁷The teachers of the law and the Pharisees were watching closely to see if Jesus would heal on the Sabbath day so they could accuse him. ⁸But he knew what they were thinking, and he said to the man with the crippled hand, "Stand up here in the middle of everyone." The man got up and stood there. ⁹Then Jesus said to them, "I ask you, which is lawful on the Sabbath day: to do good or to do evil, to save a life or to destroy it?"¹⁰Jesus looked around at all of them and said to the man, "Hold out your hand." The man held out his hand, and it was healed.

¹¹But the Pharisees and the teachers of the law were very angry and discussed with each other what they could do to Jesus.

¹²At that time Jesus went off to a mountain to pray, and he spent the night praying to God. ¹³The next morning, Jesus called his followers to him and chose twelve of them, whom he named apostles:¹⁴Simon (Jesus named him Peter), his brother Andrew, James, John, Philip, Bartholomew, ¹⁵Matthew, Thomas, James son of Alphaeus, Simon (called the Zealot), ¹⁶Judas son of James, and Judas Iscariot, who later turned Jesus over to his enemies.

NKJV

him, which is not lawful for any but the priests to eat?"⁵And He said to them, "The Son of Man is also Lord of the Sabbath."

⁶Now it happened on another Sabbath, also, that He entered the synagogue and taught. And a man was there whose right hand was withered. ⁷So the scribes and Pharisees watched Him closely, whether He would heal on the Sabbath, that they might find an accusation against Him. ⁸But He knew their thoughts, and said to the man who had the withered hand, "Arise and stand here." And he arose and stood. ⁹Then Jesus said to them, "I will ask you one thing: Is it lawful on the Sabbath to do good or to do evil, to save life or to destroy?" ¹⁰And when He had looked around at them all, He said to the man, "Stretch out your hand." And he did so, and his hand was restored as whole as the other. ¹¹But they were filled with rage, and discussed with one another what they might do to Jesus.

¹²Now it came to pass in those days that He went out to the mountain to pray, and continued all night in prayer to God. ¹³And when it was day, He called His disciples to *Himself;* and from them He chose twelve whom He also named apostles: ¹⁴Simon, whom He also named Peter, and Andrew his brother; James and John; Philip and Bartholomew;¹⁵Matthew and Thomas; James the *son* of Alphaeus, and Simon called the Zealot; ¹⁶Judas *the son* of James, and Judas Iscariot who also became a traitor.

DISCOVERY

Explore the Bible reading by discussing these questions.

2. What kind of power struggles did Jesus have with the religious leaders of his day?

_____

_____

_____

3. How did Jesus deal with the accusations of the Pharisees and teachers of the law?

_____

_____

_____

4. Why did Jesus' actions enrage the religious leaders?

_____

_____

_____

5. In what way did Jesus cope with the pressures of his ministry?

_____

_____

_____

6. Why did Jesus spend the night in prayer before choosing the twelve disciples?

_____

_____

_____

INSPIRATION

Here is an uplifting thought from *The Inspirational Bible*.

"He went up on a mountainside by Himself to pray." ...

Maybe he didn't ask for anything. Maybe he just stood quietly in the presence of Presence and basked in the Majesty. Perhaps he placed his war-weary self before the throne and rested.

Maybe he lifted his head out of the confusion of earth long enough to hear the solution of heaven. Perhaps he was reminded that hard hearts don't faze the Father. That problem people don't perturb the Eternal One.

We don't know what he did or what he said. But we do know the result. The hill became a steppingstone; the storm became a path. And the disciples saw Jesus as they had never seen him before.

During the storm, Jesus prayed. The sky darkened. The winds howled. Yet he prayed. The people grumbled. The disciples doubted. Yet he prayed. When forced to choose between the muscles of men and the mountain of prayer, he prayed.

Jesus did not try to do it by himself. Why should you?

There are crevasses in your life that you cannot cross alone. There are hearts in your world that you cannot change without help. There are mountains that you cannot climb until you climb his mountain.

Climb it. You will be amazed.

(From *In the Eye of the Storm*
by Max Lucado)

RESPONSE

Use these questions to share more deeply with each other.

7. What lessons can we learn from Jesus' spiritual habits while he lived on earth?

_____

_____

_____

8. List some benefits of extended times of prayer.

_____

_____

_____

9. In what way does Jesus' example inspire you to change the way you deal with the pressures of your job or ministry?

_____

_____

_____

PRAYER

Lord, help us to follow in your footsteps. Teach us to pray, during times of joy or heartache, confusion or calm. When we face difficult decisions, help us to turn to you for guidance. And when life is easy, keep us from thinking that we can make it on our own. Remind us that only you can help us live victoriously.

JOURNALING

Take a few moments to record your personal insights from this lesson.

When can I spend an extended time praying about a specific decision or challenge in my life?

ADDITIONAL QUESTIONS

10. Why is prayer essential to effective ministry?

_____

_____

_____

11. What happens when we try to do God's work in our own strength?

_____

_____

_____

12. What practical steps can you take to depend more on God to help you face the challenges in your life?

_____

_____

_____

For more Bible passages on the benefits of prayer, see Deuteronomy 4:7; 2 Chronicles 7:14; Matthew 21:22; Mark 11:22–26; Acts 10:2–5; Philippians 4:6–7; 1 Timothy 4:4–5; James 5:13–18.

To complete the Book of Luke during this twelve-part study, read Luke 6:1–49.

ADDITIONAL THOUGHTS

LESSON FOUR

CHRIST'S COMPASSION

REFLECTION

Begin your study by sharing thoughts on this question.

1. Think of a time when someone showed compassion to you. Describe how this made you feel.

_____

_____

_____

BIBLE READING

Read Luke 7:11–23 from the NCV or the NKJV.

NCV

¹¹Soon afterwards Jesus went to a town called Nain, and his followers and a large crowd traveled with him. ¹²When he came near the town gate, he saw a funeral. A mother, who was a widow, had lost her only son. A large crowd from the town was with the mother while her son was being carried out. ¹³When the Lord saw her, he felt very sorry for her and said, "Don't cry." ¹⁴He went up and touched the coffin, and the people who were carrying it stopped. Jesus said, "Young man, I tell you, get up!" ¹⁵And the

NKJV

¹¹Now it happened, the day after, *that* He went into a city called Nain; and many of His disciples went with Him, and a large crowd. ¹²And when He came near the gate of the city, behold, a dead man was being carried out, the only son of his mother; and she was a widow. And a large crowd from the city was with her. ¹³When the Lord saw her, He had compassion on her and said to her, "Do not weep." ¹⁴Then He came and touched the open coffin, and those who carried *him* stood still. And He said,

son sat up and began to talk. Then Jesus gave him back to his mother.

¹⁶All the people were amazed and began praising God, saying, "A great prophet has come to us! God has come to help his people."

¹⁷This news about Jesus spread through all Judea and into all the places around there.

¹⁸John's followers told him about all these things. He called for two of his followers ¹⁹and sent them to the Lord to ask, "Are you the One who is to come, or should we wait for someone else?"

²⁰When the men came to Jesus, they said, "John the Baptist sent us to you with this question: 'Are you the One who is to come, or should we wait for someone else?'"

²¹At that time, Jesus healed many people of their sicknesses, diseases, and evil spirits, and he gave sight to many blind people. ²²Then Jesus answered John's followers, "Go tell John what you saw and heard here. The blind can see, the crippled can walk, and people with skin diseases are healed. The deaf can hear, the dead are raised to life, and the Good News is preached to the poor. ²³Those who do not stumble in their faith because of me are blessed!"

"Young man, I say to you, arise." ¹⁵So he who was dead sat up and began to speak. And He presented him to his mother.

¹⁶Then fear came upon all, and they glorified God, saying, "A great prophet has risen up among us"; and, "God has visited His people." ¹⁷And this report about Him went throughout all Judea and all the surrounding region.

¹⁸Then the disciples of John reported to him concerning all these things. ¹⁹And John, calling two of his disciples to *him,* sent *them* to Jesus, saying, "Are You the Coming One, or do we look for another?"

²⁰When the men had come to Him, they said, "John the Baptist has sent us to You, saying, 'Are You the Coming One, or do we look for another?'" ²¹And that very hour He cured many of infirmities, afflictions, and evil spirits; and to many blind He gave sight.

²²Jesus answered and said to them, "Go and tell John the things you have seen and heard: that *the* blind see, *the* lame walk, *the* lepers are cleansed, *the* deaf hear, *the* dead are raised, *the* poor have the gospel preached to them. ²³"And blessed is *he* who is not offended because of Me."

DISCOVERY

Explore the Bible reading by discussing these questions.

2. Jesus and his followers encountered a funeral procession near the city of Nain. Why do you think Jesus chose to resurrect the boy?

_____

_____

_____

3. Describe Jesus' compassion for the people in the funeral procession.

_____

_____

_____

4. In what way did Jesus specifically show his compassion for the mother who had lost her son?

_____

_____

_____

5. What good came from the miracle Jesus performed?

_____

_____

_____

6. What does it mean to stumble or be offended in our faith?

_____

_____

_____

INSPIRATION

Here is an uplifting thought from *The Inspirational Bible.*

Two crowds. One entering the city and one leaving. They couldn't be more diverse. The group arriving buzzes with laughter and conversation. They follow Jesus. The group leaving the city is solemn—a herd of sadness hypnotized by the requiem of death. Above them rides the reason for their grief—a cold body on a wicker stretcher.

The woman at the back of the procession is the mother. She has walked this trail before. It seems like just yesterday she buried the body of her husband. Her son walked with her then. Now she walks alone, quarantined in her sadness. She is the victim of this funeral.

She is the one with no arm around her shoulder. She is the one who will sleep in the empty house tonight. She is the one who will make dinner for one and conversation with none. She is the one most violated. The thief stole her most treasured diamond—companionship.

The followers of Jesus stop and step aside as

the procession shadows by. The blanket of mourning muffles the laughter of the disciples. No one spoke. What could they say? . . .

Jesus, however, knew what to say and what to do. When he saw the mother, his heart began to break . . . and his lips began to tighten. He glared at the angel of death that hovered over the body of the boy. "Not this time, Satan. This boy is mine."

At that moment the mother walked in front of him. Jesus spoke to her. "Don't cry." She stopped and looked into this stranger's face. If she wasn't shocked by his presumption, you can bet some of the witnesses were.

Don't cry? Don't cry? What kind of request is that?

A request only God can make.

Jesus stepped toward the bier and touched it. The pall-bearers stopped marching. The mourners ceased moaning. As Jesus stared at the boy, the crowd was silent. . . .

Jesus turned his attention to the dead boy. "Young man," his voice was calm, "come back to life again."

The living stood motionless as the dead came to life. Wooden fingers moved. Gray-pale cheeks blushed. The dead man sat up. . . .

Jesus must have smiled as the two embraced. Stunned, the crowd broke into cheers and applause. They hugged each other and slapped Jesus on the back. Someone proclaimed the undeniable, "God has come to help his people."

Jesus gave the woman much more than her son. He gave her a secret—a whisper that was overheard by us. "That," he said pointing at the cot, "that is fantasy. This," he grinned, putting an arm around the boy, "this is reality."

(From *Six Hours One Friday*
by Max Lucado)

RESPONSE

Use these questions to share more deeply with each other.

7. What do you think motivated Jesus to heal the sick, deliver the demon-possessed, and give sight to the blind?

_____

_____

_____

8. What new insight can you gain from this passage about Christ's character?

_____

_____

_____

9. What difference does it make in our lives to know that Jesus had mercy on people?

_____

_____

_____

PRAYER

Lord, thank you for taking the time to save a poor widow from a life of loneliness. It helps us see your power over death and your deep love and compassion for needy people. Our hearts overflow with gratitude for the mercy you have shown to us. Receive our praise and help us to show your love to the people around us.

JOURNALING

Take a few moments to record your personal insights from this lesson.

How has Jesus shown compassion to me?

ADDITIONAL QUESTIONS

10. What keeps us from acknowledging and appreciating what Jesus has done for us?

_____

_____

_____

11. In what tangible way can we thank Jesus for the love and mercy he has shown to us?

_____

_____

_____

12. Think of one person to whom you could show more Christian compassion. Why have you not so far?

_____

_____

_____

For more Bible passages on Christ's compassion, see Matthew 9:35–36; 14:13–14; 15:32–39; 20:29–34; Mark 1:40–42; 6:34; 8:2.

To complete the Book of Luke during this twelve-part study, read Luke 7:1–50.

LESSON FIVE

OBEYING GOD'S WORD

REFLECTION

Begin your study by sharing thoughts on this question.

1. Consider the first time you heard and understood the gospel message. What was your response?

_____

_____

_____

BIBLE READING

Read Luke 8:4–15 from the NCV or the NKJV.

NCV

⁴When a great crowd was gathered, and people were coming to Jesus from every town, he told them this story:

⁵"A farmer went out to plant his seed. While he was planting, some seed fell by the road. People walked on the seed, and the birds ate it up. ⁶Some seed fell on rock, and when it began to grow, it died because it had no water. ⁷Some seed fell among thorny weeds, but the weeds grew up with it and choked the good plants. ⁸And some seed fell on good ground and grew

NKJV

⁴And when a great multitude had gathered, and they had come to Him from every city, He spoke by a parable:⁵"A sower went out to sow his seed. And as he sowed, some fell by the wayside; and it was trampled down, and the birds of the air devoured it. ⁶Some fell on rock; and as soon as it sprang up, it withered away because it lacked moisture. ⁷And some fell among thorns, and the thorns sprang up with it and choked it. ⁸But others fell on good ground, sprang up, and yielded a crop a

NCV

and made a hundred times more."

As Jesus finished the story, he called out, "You people who can hear me, listen!"

⁹Jesus' followers asked him what this story meant.

¹⁰Jesus said, "You have been chosen to know the secrets about the kingdom of God. But I use stories to speak to other people so that:

'They will look, but they may not see.

They will listen, but they may not

understand.'   *Isaiah* 6:9

¹¹"This is what the story means: The seed is God's message. ¹²The seed that fell beside the road is like the people who hear God's teaching, but the devil comes and takes it away from them so they cannot believe it and be saved. ¹³The seed that fell on rock is like those who hear God's teaching and accept it gladly, but they don't allow the teaching to go deep into their lives. They believe for a while, but when trouble comes, they give up. ¹⁴The seed that fell among the thorny weeds is like those who hear God's teaching, but they let the worries, riches, and pleasures of this life keep them from growing and producing good fruit. ¹⁵And the seed that fell on the good ground is like those who hear God's teaching with good, honest hearts and obey it and patiently produce good fruit.

NKJV

hundredfold." When He had said these things He cried, "He who has ears to hear, let him hear!"

⁹Then His disciples asked Him, saying, "What does this parable mean?"

¹⁰And He said, "To you it has been given to know the mysteries of the kingdom of God, but to the rest *it is given* in parables, that

'Seeing they may not see,

And hearing they may not understand.'

¹¹"Now the parable is this: The seed is the word of God. ¹²Those by the wayside are the ones who hear; then the devil comes and takes away the word out of their hearts, lest they should believe and be saved. ¹³But the ones on the rock *are those* who, when they hear, receive the word with joy; and these have no root, who believe for a while and in time of temptation fall away. ¹⁴Now the ones *that* fell among thorns are those who, when they have heard, go out and are choked with cares, riches, and pleasures of life, and bring no fruit to maturity. ¹⁵But the ones *that* fell on the good ground are those who, having heard the word with a noble and good heart, keep *it* and bear fruit with patience.

DISCOVERY

Explore the Bible reading by discussing these questions.

2. Why do you think Jesus told such a mysterious story to such a large crowd?

_____

_____

_____

3. Why did Jesus use stories and parables to teach people?

_____

_____

_____

4. In the parable, what do the seed and the four soils represent?

_____

_____

_____

5. What interferes with people's acceptance of the gospel?

_____

_____

_____

6. What evidence in a person's life proves that God's Word has taken root?

_____

_____

_____

INSPIRATION

Here is an uplifting thought from *The Inspirational Bible*.

Only when I reach the point where I solemnly place great store upon what He says will it ever become a powerful force in my life.

Only when I really take Him seriously will His Word be made Spirit and life (supernatural life) to me.

Only when I recognize that what I am hearing is in fact and in truth divine revelation designed by deity for my own good, will I hear it as a Word from above.

God has chosen to articulate Himself to me as a man in four ways: through the natural created universe around me; through His Word expressed by inspired men who reported it in human language I can read and understand; through the person of Jesus Christ, the Word made flesh, exemplified in human form; through those other men and women in whom He deigns to reside by His own Gracious Spirit.

He may speak to me deliberately and distinctly through any one or all of these ways. It is my responsibility then to recognize: "O God, You are communicating with me. I will listen. I do recognize Your voice communing with me." . . .

I must set aside whatever else preoccupies my thoughts and give my undivided attention to the Lord.

It is not good enough to "half listen" to God. He demands my total concentration on what He is conveying to me. He knows that anything less will leave me halfhearted. . . .

My positive response results in immediate

action on my part. His will is done. His wishes are carried out. His desires are complied with happily. His commands are executed without delay or debate.

In short I simply do what He asks me to do.

This is faith in action—the faith of obedience.

This is the gateway into the good ground of God's garden.

This is to "hear" the Word and have it come alive.

This is to have Him implant the good seed of His good intentions for me in the good, warm, open, prepared soil of my responsive soul.

The seed will germinate. The young plants will prosper and grow vigorously. There will be fruit production of His choosing—a harvest that delights Him and refreshes others.

(From *A Gardener Looks at the Fruits of the Spirit* by Phillip Keller)

RESPONSE

Use these questions to share more deeply with each other.

7. How does God speak to us today?

_____

_____

_____

8. What prevents us from hearing and obeying the Word of God?

_____

_____

_____

9. In what ways can we increase our openness to God's Word?

_____

_____

_____

PRAYER

We cherish the precious gift of your Word, Father. We praise you for providing a way to communicate with us. Give us ears to hear your voice and hearts willing to obey. Plant your good seed in our souls. May it dig deep into our lives and produce good fruit for your kingdom.

JOURNALING

Take a few moments to record your personal insights from this lesson.

How can I become more like the good ground described in Jesus' parable?

ADDITIONAL QUESTIONS

10. What good fruit is produced when we obey God's teaching?

_____

_____

_____

11. How can the worries of life keep us from growing and producing fruit?

_____

_____

_____

12. In what ways has God's Word changed your life?

_____

_____

_____

For more Bible passages on obeying the Bible, see Leviticus 18:4–5; 25:18; Deuteronomy 6:3; 13:4; 30:10; Joshua 22:5; 1 Kings 8:61; Psalm 119:1–40; Luke 11:28; John 14:23; Romans 2:13; 1 John 3:24; 2 John 6; Revelation 14:12.

To complete the Book of Luke during this twelve-part study, read Luke 8:1–56.

LESSON SIX

BELIEVING IN JESUS

REFLECTION

Begin your study by sharing thoughts on this question.

1. How would your friends and co-workers answer the question, "Who is Jesus?"

_____

_____

_____

BIBLE READING

Read Luke 9:18–27 from the NCV or the NKJV.

NCV

¹⁸One time when Jesus was praying alone, his followers were with him, and he asked them, "Who do the people say I am?"

¹⁹They answered, "Some say you are John the Baptist. Others say you are Elijah. And others say you are one of the prophets from long ago who has come back to life."

²⁰Then Jesus asked, "But who do you say I am?"

Peter answered, "You are the Christ from God."

NKJV

¹⁸And it happened, as He was alone praying, *that* His disciples joined Him, and He asked them, saying, "Who do the crowds say that I am?"

¹⁹So they answered and said, "John the Baptist, but some *say* Elijah; and others *say* that one of the old prophets has risen again."

²⁰He said to them, "But who do you say that I am?"

Peter answered and said, "The Christ of God."

NCV

²¹Jesus warned them not to tell anyone, saying, ²²"The Son of Man must suffer many things. He will be rejected by the older Jewish leaders, the leading priests, and the teachers of the law. He will be killed and after three days will be raised from the dead."

²³Jesus said to all of them, "If people want to follow me, they must give up the things they want. They must be willing to give up their lives daily to follow me. ²⁴Those who want to save their lives will give up true life. But those who give up their lives for me will have true life. ²⁵It is worth nothing for them to have the whole world if they themselves are destroyed or lost. ²⁶If people are ashamed of me and my teaching, then the Son of Man will be ashamed of them when he comes in his glory and with the glory of the Father and the holy angels. ²⁷I tell you the truth, some people standing here will see the kingdom of God before they die."

NKJV

²¹And He strictly warned and commanded them to tell this to no one, ²²saying, "The Son of Man must suffer many things, and be rejected by the elders and chief priests and scribes, and be killed, and be raised the third day."

²³Then He said to *them* all, "If anyone desires to come after Me, let him deny himself, and take up his cross daily, and follow Me. ²⁴For whoever desires to save his life will lose it, but whoever loses his life for My sake will save it. ²⁵For what profit is it to a man if he gains the whole world, and is himself destroyed or lost? ²⁶For whoever is ashamed of Me and My words, of him the Son of Man will be ashamed when He comes in His *own* glory, and *in His* Father's, and of the holy angels. ²⁷But I tell you truly, there are some standing here who shall not taste death till they see the kingdom of God."

DISCOVERY

Explore the Bible reading by discussing these questions.

2. Why do you think Jesus posed probing questions to his disciples about his identity?

_____

_____

_____

3. What different views did people have about Jesus' identity?

_____

_____

_____

4. Why did Jesus warn the disciples to keep his true identity a secret?

_____

_____

_____

5. What kind of commitment does Jesus require from his followers?

_____

_____

_____

6. List the rewards of sacrificing one's life to follow Jesus.

_____

_____

_____

INSPIRATION

Here is an uplifting thought from *The Inspirational Bible*.

One of the most dramatic scenes in the New Testament occurred in a city known as Caesarea Phillipi. . . . It was indeed a dramatic picture. In the midst of this carnival of marble columns and golden idols, a penniless, homeless, nameless Nazarene asks his band of followers, "Who do you say that I am?"

The immensity of the question is staggering. I would imagine that Peter's answer did not come without some hesitation. Shuffling of feet. Anxious silence. How absurd that this man should be the Son of God. No trumpets. No purple robes. No armies. Yet there was that glint of determination in his eye and that edge of certainty in his message. Peter's response sliced the silence. "I believe that you are . . . the Son of God."

Many have looked at Jesus; but few have seen him. Many have seen his shadow, his people, his story. But only a handful have seen Jesus. Only a few have looked through the fog of religiosity and found him. Only a few have dared to stand eye to eye and heart to heart with Jesus and say, "I believe that you are the Son of God."

(From *On the Anvil* by Max Lucado)

RESPONSE

Use these questions to share more deeply with each other.

7. Why is Jesus' identity crucial to your faith?

_____

_____

_____

8. How would you explain what you believe about Jesus to a person who had never heard his name?

_____

_____

_____

9. Explain what it means to give up your life daily to follow Jesus.

_____

_____

_____

PRAYER

Lord Jesus, we believe that you are the Son of God. We want to follow you, but sometimes we are scared of the risks and costs involved. But your Word teaches us that any sacrifice we make will be well worth the eternal reward. So we ask you to take our focus off of the things of this world and set our hopes on spending eternity with you.

JOURNALING

Take a few moments to record your personal insights from this lesson.

What things do I need to give up to follow Jesus wholeheartedly?

ADDITIONAL QUESTIONS

10. What opportunities have you had to proclaim your faith in Jesus?

_____

_____

_____

11. In what circumstances is it difficult for you to share your religious views?

_____

_____

_____

12. In what way does this passage motivate you to speak out about your faith in Jesus Christ?

_____

_____

_____

For more Bible passages on believing in Jesus, see John 3:14–18; 4:42; 8:24; 9:35–38; 13:19–20; 16:30–31; 20:24–31; Acts 16:31; 19:4; Romans 3:22; 10:14; Philippians 1:29; 1 Thessalonians 4:14; 1 John 5:1–12.

To complete the Book of Luke during this twelve-part study, read Luke 9:1–10:42.

ADDITIONAL THOUGHTS

LESSON SEVEN

PERSISTENT PRAYER

REFLECTION

Begin your study by sharing thoughts on this question.

1. Think of a time when you felt like giving up on a certain prayer request. What helped you keep on praying?

_____

_____

_____

BIBLE READING

Read Luke 11:1–13 from the NCV or the NKJV.

NCV

¹One time Jesus was praying in a certain place. When he finished, one of his followers said to him, "Lord, teach us to pray as John taught his followers."

²Jesus said to them, "When you pray, say:
'Father, may your name always be kept holy.
May your kingdom come.
³Give us the food we need for each day.
⁴Forgive us for our sins,
   because we forgive everyone who has
      done wrong to us.
And do not cause us to be tempted.'"

NKJV

Now it came to pass, as He was praying in a certain place, when He ceased, *that* one of His disciples said to Him, "Lord, teach us to pray, as John also taught his disciples."

²So He said to them, "When you pray, say:

   Our Father in heaven,
   Hallowed be Your name.
   Your kingdom come.
   Your will be done
   On earth as *it is* in heaven.
³ Give us day by day our daily bread.

NCV

⁵Then Jesus said to them, "Suppose one of you went to your friend's house at midnight and said to him, 'Friend, loan me three loaves of bread. ⁶A friend of mine has come into town to visit me, but I have nothing for him to eat.' ⁷Your friend inside the house answers, 'Don't bother me! The door is already locked, and my children and I are in bed. I cannot get up and give you anything.' ⁸I tell you, if friendship is not enough to make him get up to give you the bread, your boldness will make him get up and give you whatever you need. ⁹So I tell you, ask, and God will give to you. Search, and you will find. Knock, and the door will open for you. ¹⁰Yes, everyone who asks will receive. The one who searches will find. And everyone who knocks will have the door opened. ¹¹If your children ask for a fish, which of you would give them a snake instead? ¹²Or, if your children ask for an egg, would you give them a scorpion? ¹³Even though you are bad, you know how to give good things to your children. How much more your heavenly Father will give the Holy Spirit to those who ask him!"

NKJV

⁴ And forgive us our sins,
  For we also forgive everyone who is
    indebted to us.
  And do not lead us into temptation,
  But deliver us from the evil one.' "

⁵And He said to them, "Which of you shall have a friend, and go to him at midnight and say to him, 'Friend, lend me three loaves; ⁶for a friend of mine has come to me on his journey, and I have nothing to set before him'; ⁷and he will answer from within and say, 'Do not trouble me; the door is now shut, and my children are with me in bed; I cannot rise and give to you'? ⁸I say to you, though he will not rise and give to him because he is his friend, yet because of his persistence he will rise and give him as many as he needs.

⁹"So I say to you, ask, and it will be given to you; seek, and you will find; knock, and it will be opened to you. ¹⁰For everyone who asks receives, and he who seeks finds, and to him who knocks it will be opened. ¹¹If a son asks for bread from any father among you, will he give him a stone? Or if *he asks* for a fish, will he give him a serpent instead of a fish? ¹²Or if he asks for an egg, will he offer him a scorpion? ¹³If you then, being evil, know how to give good gifts to your children, how much more will *your* heavenly Father give the Holy Spirit to those who ask Him!"

DISCOVERY

Explore the Bible reading by discussing these questions.

2. Why do you think Jesus' act of prayer sparked the disciples' interest in prayer?

_____

_____

_____

3. List several elements of prayer.

_____

_____

_____

4. In Jesus' story of the friend in need of bread, who do the two friends represent?

_____

_____

_____

5. What spiritual principles did Jesus convey to his disciples through his daily example and teaching?

_____

_____

_____

6. Why is persistence in prayer important?

_____

_____

_____

INSPIRATION

Here is an uplifting thought from *The Inspirational Bible.*

One of my favorite stories concerns a bishop who was traveling by ship to visit a church across the ocean. While en route, the ship stopped at an island for a day. He went for a walk on a beach. He came upon three fishermen mending their nets.

Curious about their trade he asked them some questions. Curious about his ecclesiastical robes, they asked him some questions. When they found out he was a Christian leader, they got excited. "We Christians!" they said, proudly pointing to one another.

The bishop was impressed but cautious. Did they know the Lord's Prayer? They had never heard of it.

"What do you say, then, when you pray?"

"We pray, 'O We are three, you are three, have mercy on us.'"

The bishop was appalled at the primitive nature of the prayer. "That will not do." So he spent the day teaching them the Lord's Prayer. The fishermen were poor but willing learners. And before the bishop sailed away the next day, they could recite the prayer with no mistakes.

The bishop was proud.

On the return trip the bishop's ship drew near the island again. When the island came into view the bishop came to the deck and recalled with pleasure the men he had taught and resolved to go see them again. As he was thinking a light appeared on the horizon near the island. It seemed to be getting nearer. As the bishop gazed in wonder he realized the three fishermen were walking toward him on the water. Soon all the passengers and crew were on the deck to see the sight.

When they were within speaking distance, the fisherman cried out, "Bishop, we come hurry to meet you."

"What is it you want?" asked the stunned bishop.

"We are so sorry. We forget lovely prayer. We say, 'O Our Father, who art in heaven, hallowed be your name . . .' and then we forget. Please tell us prayer again."

The bishop was humbled. "Go back to your homes, my friends, and when you pray say, 'O We are three, you are three, have mercy on us.'"

(From *And the Angels Were Silent* by Max Lucado)

RESPONSE

Use these questions to share more deeply with each other.

7. In what way does the Lord's prayer serve as a model for us to follow?

_____

_____

_____

8. What are the dangers of reciting the same prayers over and over?

_____

_____

_____

9. What steps can we take to keep our prayers honest and meaningful?

_____

_____

_____

PRAYER

Father, forgive us for giving up on prayer so easily. Forgive us for our insincerity and lack of interest. We thank you for remaining faithful to us, even when we are unfaithful. Teach us how to pray honestly, persistently, and faithfully. Most importantly, Father, help us to follow in the footsteps of your perfect Son, Jesus Christ.

JOURNALING

Take a few moments to record your personal insights from this lesson.

What is one principle I can apply from this passage to strengthen my prayer life?

ADDITIONAL QUESTIONS

10. In what circumstances is it tempting to give up praying?

_____

_____

_____

11. What can persistent prayer accomplish?

_____

_____

_____

12. In what way does this passage change your attitude toward a long-term prayer request or need in your life?

_____

_____

_____

For more Bible passages on prayer, see 1 Chronicles 5:20; Matthew 17:20; 21:21–22; Luke 17:6; 18:40–42; Romans 12:12; Ephesians 6:18; James 5:15–16; Jude 20.

To complete the Book of Luke during this twelve-part study, read Luke 11:1–54.

LESSON EIGHT

TRUSTING GOD

REFLECTION

Begin your study by sharing thoughts on this idea.

1. Describe a time when God met one of your needs in an unexpected or unusual way.

_____

_____

_____

BIBLE READING

Read Luke 12:22–34 from the NCV or the NKJV.

NCV

²²Jesus said to his followers, "So I tell you, don't worry about the food you need to live, or about the clothes you need for your body. ²³Life is more than food, and the body is more than clothes. ²⁴Look at the birds. They don't plant or harvest, they don't have storerooms or barns, but God feeds them. And you are worth much more than birds. ²⁵You cannot add any time to your life by worrying about it. ²⁶If you cannot do even the little things, then why worry about the big things? ²⁷Consider how the lilies grow;

NKJV

²²Then He said to His disciples, "Therefore I say to you, do not worry about your life, what you will eat; nor about the body, what you will put on. ²³Life is more than food, and the body *is more* than clothing. ²⁴Consider the ravens, for they neither sow nor reap, which have neither storehouse nor barn; and God feeds them. Of how much more value are you than the birds? ²⁵And which of you by worrying can add one cubit to his stature? ²⁶If you then are not able to do *the* least, why are you anxious for

NCV

they don't work or make clothes for themselves. But I tell you that even Solomon with his riches was not dressed as beautifully as one of these flowers. 28God clothes the grass in the field, which is alive today but tomorrow is thrown into the fire. So how much more will God clothe you? Don't have so little faith! 29Don't always think about what you will eat or what you will drink, and don't keep worrying. 30All the people in the world are trying to get these things, and your Father knows you need them. 31But seek God's kingdom, and all the other things you need will be given to you.

32"Don't fear, little flock, because your Father wants to give you the kingdom. 33Sell your possessions and give to the poor. Get for yourselves purses that will not wear out, the treasure in heaven that never runs out, where thieves can't steal and moths can't destroy. 34Your heart will be where your treasure is."

NKJV

the rest? 27Consider the lilies, how they grow: they neither toil nor spin; and yet I say to you, even Solomon in all his glory was not arrayed like one of these. 28If then God so clothes the grass, which today is in the field and tomorrow is thrown into the oven, how much more *will He clothe* you, O *you* of little faith?

29"And do not seek what you should eat or what you should drink, nor have an anxious mind. 30For all these things the nations of the world seek after, and your Father knows that you need these things. 31But seek the kingdom of God, and all these things shall be added to you.

32"Do not fear, little flock, for it is your Father's good pleasure to give you the kingdom. 33Sell what you have and give alms; provide yourselves money bags which do not grow old, a treasure in the heavens that does not fail, where no thief approaches nor moth destroys. 34For where your treasure is, there your heart will be also."

DISCOVERY

Explore the Bible reading by discussing these questions.

2. Why should believers trust God, instead of worrying?

_____

_____

_____

3. Jesus gave two examples from nature about trusting God: sparrows and lilies. Can you think of any others?

_____

_____

_____

4. Explain how worry demonstrates a lack of faith.

_____

_____

_____

5. What are the rewards of seeking God's kingdom, instead of personal gain?

_____

_____

_____

6. How do earthly riches differ from heavenly treasure?

_____

_____

_____

INSPIRATION

Here is an uplifting thought from *The Inspirational Bible.*

Be honest. Are we glad he says no to what we want and yes to what we need? Not always. If we ask for a new marriage, and he says honor the one you've got, we aren't happy. If we ask for healing, and he says learn through the pain, we aren't happy. If we ask for more money, and he says treasure the unseen, we aren't always happy.

When God doesn't do what we want, it's not easy. Never has been. Never will be. But faith is the conviction that God knows more than we do about this life and he will get us through it.

Remember, disappointment is caused by unmet expectations. Disappointment is cured by revamped expectations.

I like that story about the fellow who went to the pet store in search of a singing parakeet. Seems he was a bachelor and his house was too quiet. The store owner had just the bird for him, so the man bought it. The next day the bachelor came home from work to a house full of music. He went to the cage to feed the bird and noticed for the first time that the parakeet had only one leg.

He felt cheated that he'd been sold a one-legged bird, so he called and complained.

"What do you want," the store owner responded, "a bird who can sing or a bird who can dance?" . . .

We need to hear that God is still in control. We need to hear that it's not over until he says so. We need to hear that life's mishaps and tragedies are not a reason to bail out. They are simply a reason to sit tight.

Corrie ten Boom used to say, "When the train goes through a tunnel and the world gets dark, do you jump out? Of course not. You sit still and trust the engineer to get you through." . . .

Next time you're disappointed, don't panic. Don't jump out. Don't give up. Just be patient and let God remind you he's still in control. It ain't over till it's over.

(From *He Still Moves Stones*
by Max Lucado)

RESPONSE

Use these questions to share more deeply with each other.

7. What is the secret of contentment?

_____

_____

_____

8. List some of the consequences of anxiety.

_____

_____

_____

9. What simple steps can believers take to avoid worry?

_____

_____

_____

PRAYER

Father, your Word promises that you will protect and provide for your people. Forgive us for choosing to worry instead of depending on you. Help us see the futility of worry and the benefits of trusting you. Calm our fears and fill us with faith so we can focus our attention and energy on seeking your kingdom.

JOURNALING

Take a few moments to record your personal insights from this lesson.

When is it most difficult for me to trust God? Why?

ADDITIONAL QUESTIONS

10. What is the difference between planning ahead and worrying?

_____

_____

_____

11. How does this passage inspire you to trust God with your needs?

_____

_____

_____

12. In what concrete ways can we demonstrate our trust in God's provision?

_____

_____

_____

For more Bible passages on trusting God, see Psalm 4:5; 20:7; 22:9–10; 37:3–5; 40:3–4; 56:3–11; 115:9–11; 125:1; Isaiah 26:4; Jeremiah 17:5–8; Daniel 6:23; Nahum 1:7; Zephaniah 3:12; John 14:1; Romans 9:33.

To complete the Book of Luke during this twelve-part study, read Luke 12:1–14:35.

ADDITIONAL THOUGHTS

LESSON NINE

GOD'S LOVE FOR PEOPLE

REFLECTION

Begin your study by sharing thoughts on this question.

1. In what tangible ways have you felt God's love for you?

_____

_____

_____

BIBLE READING

Read Luke 15:11–32 from the NCV or the NKJV.

NCV

¹¹Then Jesus said, "A man had two sons. ¹²The younger son said to his father, 'Give me my share of the property.' So the father divided the property between his two sons. ¹³Then the younger son gathered up all that was his and traveled far away to another country. There he wasted his money in foolish living. ¹⁴After he had spent everything, a time came when there was no food anywhere in the country, and the son was poor and hungry. ¹⁵So he got a job with one of the citizens there who sent the son

NKJV

¹¹Then He said: "A certain man had two sons. ¹²And the younger of them said to *his* father, 'Father, give me the portion of goods that falls *to me.*' So he divided to them *his* livelihood. ¹³And not many days after, the younger son gathered all together, journeyed to a far country, and there wasted his possessions with prodigal living. ¹⁴But when he had spent all, there arose a severe famine in that land, and he began to be in want. ¹⁵Then he went and joined himself to a citizen of that country,

NCV

into the fields to feed pigs. [16]The son was so hungry that he wanted to eat the pods the pigs were eating, but no one gave him anything. [17]When he realized what he was doing, he thought, 'All of my father's servants have plenty of food. But I am here, almost dying with hunger. [18]I will leave and return to my father and say to him, "Father, I have sinned against God and have done wrong to you. [19]I am no longer worthy to be called your son, but let me be like one of your servants."' [20]So the son left and went to his father.

"While the son was still a long way off, his father saw him and felt sorry for his son. So the father ran to him and hugged and kissed him. [21]The son said, 'Father, I have sinned against God and have done wrong to you. I am no longer worthy to be called your son.' [22]But the father said to his servants, 'Hurry! Bring the best clothes and put them on him. Also, put a ring on his finger and sandals on his feet. [23]And get our fat calf and kill it so we can have a feast and celebrate. [24]My son was dead, but now he is alive again! He was lost, but now he is found!' So they began to celebrate.

[25]"The older son was in the field, and as he came closer to the house, he heard the sound of music and dancing. [26]So he called to one of the servants and asked what all this meant. [27]The servant said, 'Your brother has come back, and your father killed the fat calf, because your brother came home safely.' [28]The older son was angry and would not go in to the feast. So his father went out and begged him to come in. [29]But the older son said to his father, 'I have served you like a slave for many years and have

NKJV

and he sent him into his fields to feed swine. [16]And he would gladly have filled his stomach with the pods that the swine ate, and no one gave him *anything.*

[17]"But when he came to himself, he said, 'How many of my father's hired servants have bread enough and to spare, and I perish with hunger! [18]I will arise and go to my father, and will say to him, "Father, I have sinned against heaven and before you, [19]and I am no longer worthy to be called your son. Make me like one of your hired servants."'

[20]"And he arose and came to his father. But when he was still a great way off, his father saw him and had compassion, and ran and fell on his neck and kissed him. [21]And the son said to him, 'Father, I have sinned against heaven and in your sight, and am no longer worthy to be called your son.' [22]"But the father said to his servants, 'Bring out the best robe and put *it* on him, and put a ring on his hand and sandals on *his* feet. [23]And bring the fatted calf here and kill *it,* and let us eat and be merry; [24]for this my son was dead and is alive again; he was lost and is found.' And they began to be merry.

[25]"Now his older son was in the field. And as he came and drew near to the house, he heard music and dancing. [26]So he called one of the servants and asked what these things meant. [27]And he said to him, 'Your brother has come, and because he has received him safe and sound, your father has killed the fatted calf.' [28]"But he was angry and would not go in. Therefore his father came out and pleaded with him. [29]So he answered and said to *his* father, 'Lo,

NCV

always obeyed your commands. But you never gave me even a young goat to have at a feast with my friends. ³⁰But your other son, who wasted all your money on prostitutes, comes home, and you kill the fat calf for him!' ³¹The father said to him, 'Son, you are always with me, and all that I have is yours. ³²We had to celebrate and be happy because your brother was dead, but now he is alive. He was lost, but now he is found.'"

NKJV

these many years I have been serving you; I never transgressed your commandment at any time; and yet you never gave me a young goat, that I might make merry with my friends. ³⁰But as soon as this son of yours came, who has devoured your livelihood with harlots, you killed the fatted calf for him.'

³¹"And he said to him, 'Son, you are always with me, and all that I have is yours. ³²It was right that we should make merry and be glad, for your brother was dead and is alive again, and was lost and is found.'"

DISCOVERY

Explore the Bible reading by discussing these questions.

2. Name some of God's character traits highlighted in the parable of the prodigal son.

_____

_____

_____

3. What happens when God gives people freedom to make their own choices?

_____

_____

_____

4. In what ways do we sometimes show disregard for God's authority, like the younger son in the story?

_____

_____

_____

5. Why do hard times often bring people to repentance?

_____

_____

_____

6. In what way does God respond to people who confess their sins and return to him?

_____

_____

_____

INSPIRATION

Here is an uplifting thought from *The Inspirational Bible.*

Theresa Briones is a tender, loving mother. She also has a stout left hook that she used to punch a lady in a coin laundry. Why'd she do it?

Some kids were making fun of Theresa's daughter, Alicia.

Alicia is bald. Her knees are arthritic. Her nose is pinched. Her hips are creaky. Her hearing is bad. She has the stamina of a seventy-year-old. And she is only ten.

"Mom," the kids taunted, "come and look at the monster!"

Alicia weighs only twenty-two pounds and is shorter than most preschoolers. She suffers from progeria—a genetic aging disease that strikes one child in eight million. The life expectancy of progeria victims is twenty years. There are only fifteen known cases of this disease in the world.

"She is not an alien. She is not a monster," Theresa defended. "She is just like you and me."

Mentally, Alicia is a bubbly, fun-loving third grader. She has a long list of friends. She watches television in a toddler-sized rocking chair. She plays with Barbie dolls and teases her younger brother.

Theresa has grown accustomed to the glances and questions. She is patient with the constant curiosity. Genuine inquiries she accepts. Insensitive slanders she does not.

The mother of the finger-pointing children came to investigate. "I see 'it,'" she told the kids.

"My child is not an 'it,'" Theresa stated. Then she decked the woman.

Who could blame her? Such is the nature of parental love. Mothers and fathers have a God-given ability to love their children regardless of imperfections. Not because the parents are blind. Just the opposite. They see vividly.

Theresa sees Alicia's inability as clearly as anyone. But she also sees Alicia's value.

So does God.

God sees us with the eyes of a Father. He sees our defects, errors, and blemishes. But he also sees our value. . . . What did Jesus know that enabled him to do what he did?

Here's part of the answer. He knew the value of people. He knew that each human being is a treasure. And because he did, people were not a source of stress, but a source of joy.

(From *In the Eye of the Storm*
by Max Lucado)

RESPONSE

Use these questions to share more deeply with each other.

7. Why does God accept and forgive sinful people?

_____

_____

_____

8. Why is it important to realize that God values all people equally?

_____

_____

_____

9. How does it feel to know that God sees all of your faults and still loves you?

_____

_____

_____

PRAYER

We stand in awe, Father, of your great love—love so deep that you sacrificed your only Son to save sinful people. Forgive us for our rebellion and disobedience. Give us the strength to turn away from our sin and accept your forgiveness. And we ask you, Father, to help us see others through your loving eyes.

JOURNALING

Take a few moments to record your personal insights from this lesson.

How can I thank God for treating me better than I deserve?

ADDITIONAL QUESTIONS

10. Why do we tend to treat some people better than others?

_____

_____

_____

11. In what ways can we combat our tendency to withhold love from certain people?

_____

_____

_____

12. Think of one person who is difficult to love. In what ways can you show God's love to that person?

_____

_____

_____

For more Bible passages on God's love for us, see Deuteronomy 7:8; Jeremiah 31:3; John 3:16; Romans 5:8; Ephesians 2:4–5; 1 John 3:1; 4:7–21.

To complete the Book of Luke during this twelve-part study, read Luke 15:1—18:43.

LESSON TEN

TRUE WORSHIP

REFLECTION

Begin your study by sharing thoughts on this question.

1. If Jesus were to visit your church this Sunday, do you think he would feel comfortable there?

_____

_____

_____

BIBLE READING

Read Luke 19:28–48 from the NCV or the NKJV.

NCV

28After Jesus said this, he went on toward Jerusalem. 29As Jesus came near Bethphage and Bethany, towns near the hill called the Mount of Olives, he sent out two of his followers. 30He said, "Go to the town you can see there. When you enter it, you will find a colt tied there, which no one has ever ridden. Untie it and bring it here to me. 31If anyone asks you why you are untying it, say that the Master needs it."

32The two followers went into town and found the colt just as Jesus had told them. 33As

NKJV

28When He had said this, He went on ahead, going up to Jerusalem. 29And it came to pass, when He came near to Bethphage and Bethany, at the mountain called Olivet, *that* He sent two of His disciples, 30saying, "Go into the village opposite *you,* where as you enter you will find a colt tied, on which no one has ever sat. Loose it and bring *it here.* 31And if anyone asks you, 'Why are you loosing *it?*' thus you shall say to him, 'Because the Lord has need of it.'"

32So those who were sent went their way and

NCV

they were untying it, its owners came out and asked the followers, "Why are you untying our colt?"

³⁴The followers answered, "The Master needs it."³⁵So they brought it to Jesus, threw their coats on the colt's back, and put Jesus on it. ³⁶As Jesus rode toward Jerusalem, others spread their coats on the road before him.

³⁷As he was coming close to Jerusalem, on the way down the Mount of Olives, the whole crowd of followers began joyfully shouting praise to God for all the miracles they had seen. ³⁸They said,

"God bless the king who comes in the
name of the Lord!   *Psalm* 118:26
There is peace in heaven and glory to God!"

³⁹Some of the Pharisees in the crowd said to Jesus, "Teacher, tell your followers not to say these things."

⁴⁰But Jesus answered, "I tell you, if my followers didn't say these things, then the stones would cry out."

⁴¹As Jesus came near Jerusalem, he saw the city and cried for it, ⁴²saying, "I wish you knew today what would bring you peace. But now it is hidden from you. ⁴³The time is coming when your enemies will build a wall around you and will hold you in on all sides. ⁴⁴They will destroy you and all your people, and not one stone will be left on another. All this will happen because you did not recognize the time when God came to save you."

⁴⁵Jesus went into the Temple and began to throw out the people who were selling things there. ⁴⁶He said, "It is written in the Scriptures, 'My Temple will be a house for prayer.' But

NKJV

found *it* just as He had said to them. ³³But as they were loosing the colt, the owners of it said to them, "Why are you loosing the colt?"

³⁴And they said, "The Lord has need of him."³⁵Then they brought him to Jesus. And they threw their own clothes on the colt, and they set Jesus on him. ³⁶And as He went, *many* spread their clothes on the road.

³⁷Then, as He was now drawing near the descent of the Mount of Olives, the whole multitude of the disciples began to rejoice and praise God with a loud voice for all the mighty works they had seen, ³⁸saying:

" 'Blessed *is* the King who comes in the
name of the LORD!'
Peace in heaven and glory in the highest!"

³⁹And some of the Pharisees called to Him from the crowd, "Teacher, rebuke Your disciples."

⁴⁰But He answered and said to them, "I tell you that if these should keep silent, the stones would immediately cry out."

⁴¹Now as He drew near, He saw the city and wept over it, ⁴²saying, "If you had known, even you, especially in this your day, the things *that make* for your peace! But now they are hidden from your eyes. ⁴³For days will come upon you when your enemies will build an embankment around you, surround you and close you in on every side, ⁴⁴and level you, and your children within you, to the ground; and they will not leave in you one stone upon another, because you did not know the time of your visitation."

⁴⁵Then He went into the temple and began

NCV

you have changed it into a 'hideout for robbers'!"

[47]Jesus taught in the Temple every day. The leading priests, the experts on the law, and some of the leaders of the people wanted to kill Jesus. [48]But they did not know how they could do it, because all the people were listening closely to him.

NKJV

to drive out those who bought and sold in it, [46]saying to them, "It is written, 'My house is a house of prayer,' but you have made it a 'den of thieves.'"

[47]And He was teaching daily in the temple. But the chief priests, the scribes, and the leaders of the people sought to destroy Him, [48]and were unable to do anything; for all the people were very attentive to hear Him.

DISCOVERY

Explore the Bible reading by discussing these questions.

2. Why did the people celebrate Jesus' entrance into Jerusalem?

_____

_____

_____

3. Why did Jesus weep when he saw Jerusalem while all the people were praising him?

_____

_____

_____

4. List some reasons Jesus would not tolerate the buying and selling in the Temple.

_____

_____

_____

5. Jesus called the Temple "a house of prayer." How well does that describe our churches today?

_____

_____

_____

6. What message did Jesus send to church leaders when he cleared the Temple?

_____

_____

_____

INSPIRATION

Here is an uplifting thought from *The Inspirational Bible*.

It's tough to be let down. It's disappointing when you think someone is interested in you, only to find they are interested in your money. When salespeople do it, it's irritating—but when people of faith do it, it can be devastating.

It's a sad but true fact of the faith: religion is used for profit and prestige. When it is, there are two results: people are exploited and God is infuriated.

There's no better example of this than what happened at the temple. After he had entered the city on the back of a donkey, Jesus "went into the Temple. After he had looked at everything, since it was already late, he went out to Bethany with the twelve apostles."

Did you catch that? The first place Jesus went when he arrived in Jerusalem was the temple. . . . He walked into the temple area, looked around, and walked out.

Want to know what he saw? Then read what he did on Monday, the next morning when he returned. "Jesus went into the Temple and threw out all the people who were buying and selling there. He turned over the tables of those who were exchanging different kinds of money, and he upset the benches of those who were selling doves. Jesus said to all the people there, It is written in the Scriptures, 'My Temple will be called a house for prayer.' But you are changing it into a 'hideout for robbers.' "(Matt. 21:12,13)

What did he see? Hucksters. Faith peddlers. What lit the fire under Jesus' broiler? What was his first thought on Monday? People in the temple making a franchise out of the faith.

It was Passover week. The Passover was the highlight of the Jewish calendar. People came from all regions and many countries to be present for the celebration. Upon arriving they were obligated to meet two requirements.

First, an animal sacrifice, usually a dove. The dove had to be perfect, without blemish. The animal could be brought in from anywhere, but odds were that if you brought a sacrifice from another place, yours would be considered insufficient by the authorities in the temple. So, under the guise of keeping the sacrifice pure, the dove sellers sold doves—at their price.

Second, the people had to pay a tax, a temple tax. It was due every year. During Passover the tax had to be rendered in local currency. Knowing many foreigners would be in Jerusalem to pay the tax, money changers conveniently set up tables and offered to exchange the foreign money for local—for a modest fee, of course.

It's not difficult to see what angered Jesus. Pilgrims journeyed days to see God, to witness the holy, to worship His Majesty. But before they were taken into the presence of God, they were taken to the cleaners. What was promised and what was delivered were two different things. . . .

"I've had enough," was written all over the Messiah's face. In he stormed. Doves flapped and tables flew. People scampered and traders scattered.

This was not an impulsive show. This was not a temper tantrum. It was a deliberate act with an intentional message. Jesus had seen the money-changers the day before. He went to sleep with pictures of this midway and its barkers in his memory. And when he woke up the next morning, knowing his days were drawing to a close, he chose to make a point: "You cash in on my people and you've got me to answer to." God will never hold guiltless those who exploit the privilege of worship.

(From *And the Angels Were Silent* by Max Lucado)

RESPONSE

Use these questions to share more deeply with each other.

7. How would you define true worship?

_____

_____

_____

8. List some things that can interfere with our worship.

_____

_____

_____

9. In what ways can we determine whether our motives are pure when we go to church?

_____

_____

_____

PRAYER

Father, forgive us for our insincerity and dishonesty. We want to learn how to worship you in spirit and in truth. We need you, Father, to help us witness your holiness, bask in your glory, and feel your presence. May we truly be thankful for the privilege of worshiping you.

JOURNALING

Take a few moments to record your personal insights from this lesson.

In light of this passage, what changes do I need to make in the way that I approach worship?

ADDITIONAL QUESTIONS

10. List some ways you have seen someone misuse religion for his or her own purposes.

_____

_____

_____

11. What responsibility do we have to eliminate inappropriate activities and behavior from the church?

_____

_____

_____

12. What steps can believers take to protect the church from exploitation?

_____

_____

_____

For more Bible passages on worship, see Joshua 22:27; 1 Chronicles 16:28–29; 2 Chronicles 29:30; Psalm 95:6; Zechariah 14:17; Matthew 2:2; 28:9; John 4:24; Romans 12:1.

To complete the Book of Luke during this twelve-part study, read Luke 19:1—20:47.

ADDITIONAL THOUGHTS

LESSON ELEVEN

CHRIST'S SACRIFICE

REFLECTION

Begin your study by sharing thoughts on this question.

1. Think of a time when you gave something up for a friend. In what way did your sacrifice help that person?

_____

_____

_____

BIBLE READING

Read Luke 23:26–49 from the NCV or the NKJV.

NCV

²⁶As they led Jesus away, Simon, a man from Cyrene, was coming in from the fields. They forced him to carry Jesus' cross and to walk behind him.

²⁷A large crowd of people was following Jesus, including some women who were sad and crying for him. ²⁸But Jesus turned and said to them, "Women of Jerusalem, don't cry for me. Cry for yourselves and for your children. ²⁹The time is coming when people will say, 'Happy are the women who cannot have

NKJV

²⁶Now as they led Him away, they laid hold of a certain man, Simon a Cyrenian, who was coming from the country, and on him they laid the cross that he might bear *it* after Jesus.

²⁷And a great multitude of the people followed Him, and women who also mourned and lamented Him. ²⁸But Jesus, turning to them, said, "Daughters of Jerusalem, do not weep for Me, but weep for yourselves and for your children. ²⁹For indeed the days are coming in which they will say, 'Blessed *are* the barren, wombs

NCV

children and who have no babies to nurse.' ³⁰Then people will say to the mountains, 'Fall on us!' And they will say to the hills, 'Cover us!' ³¹If they act like this now when life is good, what will happen when bad times come?"

³²There were also two criminals led out with Jesus to be put to death. ³³When they came to a place called the Skull, the soldiers crucified Jesus and the criminals—one on his right and the other on his left. ³⁴Jesus said, "Father, forgive them, because they don't know what they are doing."

The soldiers threw lots to decide who would get his clothes. ³⁵The people stood there watching. And the leaders made fun of Jesus, saying, "He saved others. Let him save himself if he is God's Chosen One, the Christ."

³⁶The soldiers also made fun of him, coming to Jesus and offering him some vinegar. ³⁷They said, "If you are the king of the Jews, save yourself!" ³⁸At the top of the cross these words were written: THIS IS THE KING OF THE JEWS.

³⁹One of the criminals on a cross began to shout insults at Jesus: "Aren't you the Christ? Then save yourself and us."

⁴⁰But the other criminal stopped him and said, "You should fear God! You are getting the same punishment he is. ⁴¹We are punished justly, getting what we deserve for what we did. But this man has done nothing wrong." ⁴²Then he said, "Jesus, remember me when you come into your kingdom."

⁴³Jesus said to him, "I tell you the truth, today you will be with me in paradise."

⁴⁴It was about noon, and the whole land became dark until three o'clock in the after-

NKJV

that never bore, and breasts which never nursed!' ³⁰Then they will begin 'to say to the mountains, "Fall on us!" and to the hills, "Cover us!"' ³¹For if they do these things in the green wood, what will be done in the dry?"

³²There were also two others, criminals, led with Him to be put to death. ³³And when they had come to the place called Calvary, there they crucified Him, and the criminals, one on the right hand and the other on the left. ³⁴Then Jesus said, "Father, forgive them, for they do not know what they do."

And they divided His garments and cast lots. ³⁵And the people stood looking on. But even the rulers with them sneered, saying, "He saved others; let Him save Himself if He is the Christ, the chosen of God."

³⁶The soldiers also mocked Him, coming and offering Him sour wine, ³⁷and saying, "If You are the King of the Jews, save Yourself."

³⁸And an inscription also was written over Him in letters of Greek, Latin, and Hebrew:

THIS IS THE KING OF THE JEWS.

³⁹Then one of the criminals who were hanged blasphemed Him, saying, "If You are the Christ, save Yourself and us."

⁴⁰But the other, answering, rebuked him, saying, "Do you not even fear God, seeing you are under the same condemnation? ⁴¹And we indeed justly, for we receive the due reward of our deeds; but this Man has done nothing wrong." ⁴²Then he said to Jesus, "Lord, remember me when You come into Your kingdom."

⁴³And Jesus said to him, "Assuredly, I say to

NCV

noon, ⁴⁵because the sun did not shine. The curtain in the Temple was torn in two. ⁴⁶Jesus cried out in a loud voice, "Father, I give you my life." After Jesus said this, he died.

⁴⁷When the army officer there saw what happened, he praised God, saying, "Surely this was a good man!"

⁴⁸When all the people who had gathered there to watch saw what happened, they returned home, beating their chests because they were so sad. ⁴⁹But those who were close friends of Jesus, including the women who had followed him from Galilee, stood at a distance and watched.

NKJV

you, today you will be with Me in Paradise."

⁴⁴Now it was about the sixth hour, and there was darkness over all the earth until the ninth hour. ⁴⁵Then the sun was darkened, and the veil of the temple was torn in two. ⁴⁶And when Jesus had cried out with a loud voice, He said, "Father, 'into Your hands I commit My spirit.'" Having said this, He breathed His last.

⁴⁷So when the centurion saw what had happened, he glorified God, saying, "Certainly this was a righteous Man!"

⁴⁸And the whole crowd who came together to that sight, seeing what had been done, beat their breasts and returned. ⁴⁹But all His acquaintances, and the women who followed Him from Galilee, stood at a distance, watching these things.

DISCOVERY

Explore the Bible reading by discussing these questions.

2. Why was Jesus' sacrifice necessary to restore the relationship between God and man?

_____

_____

_____

3. What character traits did Jesus exhibit during the hours before his death?

_____

_____

_____

4. In what ways should believers try to imitate Christ's attitude and actions?

_____

_____

_____

5. What was the significance of the torn curtain in the Temple leading into the Holy of Holies at the time of Christ's death?

_____

_____

_____

6. Why did Jesus submit to God's plan of salvation for the world?

_____

_____

_____

INSPIRATION

Here is an uplifting thought from *The Inspirational Bible.*

The King swallowed. . . .

He looked at the Prince of Light. "The darkness will be great." He passed his hand over the spotless face of his Son. "The pain will be awful." Then he paused and looked at his darkened dominion. When he looked up, his eyes were moist. "But there is no other way."

The Son looked into the stars as he heard the answer. "Then, let it be done."

Slowly the words that would kill the Son began to come from the lips of the Father.

"Hour of death, moment of sacrifice, it is your moment. Rehearsed a million times on false altars with false lambs; the moment of truth has come. . . .

"Oh, my Son, my Child. Look up into the heavens and see my face before I turn it. Hear my voice before I silence it. Would that I could save you and them. But they don't see and they don't hear.

"The living must die so that the dying can live. The time has come to kill the Lamb." . . .

God must have wept as he performed his task. Every lie, every lure, every act done in shadows was in that cup. Slowly, hideously they were absorbed into the body of the Son. The final act of incarnation. . . .

The throne room is dark and cavernous. The eyes of the King are closed. He is resting.

In his dream he is again in the Garden. The cool of the evening floats across the river as the three walk. They speak of the Garden—of how it is, of how it will be.

"Father . . ." the Son begins. The King replays the word again. Father. Father. The word was a flower, petal-delicate, yet so easily crushed. Oh, how he longed for his children to call him Father again.

A noise snaps him from his dream. He opens his eyes and sees a transcendent figure gleaming in the doorway. "It is finished, Father. I have come home."

(From *Six Hours One Friday*
by Max Lucado)

RESPONSE

Use these questions to share more deeply with each other.

7. Explain the significance of Jesus' death on the cross.

_____

_____

_____

8. Why is it important to accept Christ's sacrifice on our behalf?

_____

_____

_____

9. For what reasons do people refuse God's gift of salvation?

_____

_____

_____

PRAYER

Lord, you were willing to suffer pain, ridicule, and even death for us. How can we ever thank you? All we can offer you is our hearts and lives. Help us to love and obey you until we meet face to face in heaven. And while we wait for that day, use us to bring others into a right relationship with you.

JOURNALING

Take a few moments to record your personal insights from this lesson.

How can I show my appreciation for what Jesus has done for me?

ADDITIONAL QUESTIONS

10. How would our lives be different if Jesus had never died and risen again?

_____

_____

_____

11. How do you feel when you think about the pain and anguish Jesus endured for you?

_____

_____

_____

12. Who is one person you can tell about Christ's work on the cross?

_____

_____

_____

For more Bible passages on Jesus' sacrifice, see Romans 3:23–26; 8:32; 1 Corinthians 5:7; Galatians 1:3–4; 2:20; Ephesians 5:2; 1 Timothy 2:5–6; Titus 2:12–14; Hebrews 7:27; 9:23–28; 10:9–18; 1 John 2:1–2; 4:10.

To complete the Book of Luke during this twelve-part study, read Luke 21:1—23:56.

LESSON TWELVE

SEEING JESUS

REFLECTION

Begin your study by sharing thoughts on this question.

1. Who helped you understand your need for a relationship with Jesus?

_____

_____

_____

BIBLE READING

Read Luke 24:13–35 from the NCV or the NKJV.

NCV

¹³That same day two of Jesus' followers were going to a town named Emmaus, about seven miles from Jerusalem. ¹⁴They were talking about everything that had happened. ¹⁵While they were talking and discussing, Jesus himself came near and began walking with them, ¹⁶but they were kept from recognizing him. ¹⁷Then he said, "What are these things you are talking about while you walk?"

The two followers stopped, looking very sad. ¹⁸The one named Cleopas answered, "Are you

NKJV

¹³Now behold, two of them were traveling that same day to a village called Emmaus, which was seven miles from Jerusalem. ¹⁴And they talked together of all these things which had happened. ¹⁵So it was, while they conversed and reasoned, that Jesus Himself drew near and went with them. ¹⁶But their eyes were restrained, so that they did not know Him.

¹⁷And He said to them, "What kind of conversation *is* this that you have with one another as you walk and are sad?"

NCV

the only visitor in Jerusalem who does not know what just happened there?"

¹⁹Jesus said to them, "What are you talking about?"

They said, "About Jesus of Nazareth. He was a prophet who said and did many powerful things before God and all the people. ²⁰Our leaders and the leading priests handed him over to be sentenced to death, and they crucified him. ²¹But we were hoping that he would free Israel. Besides this, it is now the third day since this happened. ²²And today some women among us amazed us. Early this morning they went to the tomb, ²³but they did not find his body there. They came and told us that they had seen a vision of angels who said that Jesus was alive! ²⁴So some of our group went to the tomb, too. They found it just as the women said, but they did not see Jesus."

²⁵Then Jesus said to them, "You are foolish and slow to believe everything the prophets said. ²⁶They said that the Christ must suffer these things before he enters his glory." ²⁷Then starting with what Moses and all the prophets had said about him, Jesus began to explain everything that had been written about himself in the Scriptures.

²⁸They came near the town of Emmaus, and Jesus acted as if he were going farther. ²⁹But they begged him, "Stay with us, because it is late; it is almost night." So he went in to stay with them.

³⁰When Jesus was at the table with them, he took some bread, gave thanks, divided it, and gave it to them. ³¹And then, they were allowed to recognize Jesus. But when they saw who he

NKJV

¹⁸Then the one whose name was Cleopas answered and said to Him, "Are You the only stranger in Jerusalem, and have You not known the things which happened there in these days?"

¹⁹And He said to them, "What things?"

So they said to Him, "The things concerning Jesus of Nazareth, who was a Prophet mighty in deed and word before God and all the people, ²⁰and how the chief priests and our rulers delivered Him to be condemned to death, and crucified Him. ²¹But we were hoping that it was He who was going to redeem Israel. Indeed, besides all this, today is the third day since these things happened. ²²Yes, and certain women of our company, who arrived at the tomb early, astonished us. ²³When they did not find His body, they came saying that they had also seen a vision of angels who said He was alive. ²⁴And certain of those *who were* with us went to the tomb and found *it* just as the women had said; but Him they did not see."

²⁵Then He said to them, "O foolish ones, and slow of heart to believe in all that the prophets have spoken! ²⁶Ought not the Christ to have suffered these things and to enter into His glory?" ²⁷And beginning at Moses and all the Prophets, He expounded to them in all the Scriptures the things concerning Himself.

²⁸Then they drew near to the village where they were going, and He indicated that He would have gone farther. ²⁹But they constrained Him, saying, "Abide with us, for it is toward evening, and the day is far spent." And He went in to stay with them.

³⁰Now it came to pass, as He sat at the table

NCV

was, he disappeared. [32]They said to each other, "It felt like a fire burning in us when Jesus talked to us on the road and explained the Scriptures to us."

[33]So the two followers got up at once and went back to Jerusalem. There they found the eleven apostles and others gathered. [34]They were saying, "The Lord really has risen from the dead! He showed himself to Simon."

[35]Then the two followers told what had happened on the road and how they recognized Jesus when he divided the bread.

NKJV

with them, that He took bread, blessed and broke *it,* and gave it to them. [31]Then their eyes were opened and they knew Him; and He vanished from their sight.

[32]And they said to one another, "Did not our heart burn within us while He talked with us on the road, and while He opened the Scriptures to us?" [33]So they rose up that very hour and returned to Jerusalem, and found the eleven and those *who were* with them gathered together, [34]saying, "The Lord is risen indeed, and has appeared to Simon!" [35]And they told about the things *that had happened* on the road, and how He was known to them in the breaking of bread.

DISCOVERY

Explore the Bible reading by discussing these questions.

2. List some common misconceptions about Jesus and his ministry.

_____

_____

_____

3. What prevents people from recognizing and accepting Jesus as Savior?

_____

_____

_____

4. In what different ways does Jesus reveal himself to people?

_____

_____

_____

5. Why did Jesus make himself known to some people and not to others?

_____

_____

_____

6. What role does the Holy Spirit play in helping us see Jesus?

_____

_____

_____

INSPIRATION

Here is an uplifting thought from *The Inspirational Bible.*

Jesus. The man. The bronzed Galilean who spoke with such thunderous authority and loved with such childlike humility.

The God. The one who claimed to be older than time and greater than death.

Gone is the pomp of religion; dissipated is the fog of theology. Momentarily lifted is the opaque curtain of controversy and opinion. Erased are our own blinding errors and egotism. And there he stands.

Jesus. Have you seen him? Those who first did were never the same.

"My Lord and my God!" cried Thomas.

"I have seen the Lord," exclaimed Mary Magdalene.

"We have seen his glory," declared John.

"Were not our hearts burning within us while he talked?" rejoiced the two Emmaus-bound disciples.

But Peter said it best. "We were eyewitnesses of his majesty."

His Majesty. The emperor of Judah. The soaring eagle of eternity. The noble admiral of the Kingdom. All the splendor of heaven revealed in a human body. For a period ever so brief, the doors to the throne room were open and God came near. His Majesty was seen. Heaven touched the earth and, as a result, earth can know heaven. In astounding tandem a human body housed divinity. Holiness and earthliness intertwined.

This is no run-of-the-mill messiah. His story was extraordinary. He called himself divine, yet allowed a minimum-wage Roman soldier to drive a nail into his wrist. He demanded purity, yet stood for the rights of a repentant whore. He called men to march, yet refused to allow them to call him King. He sent men into all the world, yet equipped them with only bended knees and memories of a resurrected carpenter.

We can't regard him as simply a good teacher. His claims are too outrageous to limit him to the company of Socrates or Aristotle. Nor can we categorize him as one of many prophets sent to reveal eternal truths. His own claims eliminate that possibility.

Then who is he?

Let's try to find out. Let's follow his sandalprints. Let's sit on the cold, hard floor of the cave in which he was born. Let's smell the sawdust of the carpentry shop. Let's hear his sandals slap the hard trails of Galilee. Let's sigh as we touch the healed sores of the leper. Let's smile as we see his compassion with the woman at the well. Let's cringe as we hear the hissing of hell's Satan. Let's let our voices soar with the praises of the multitudes. Let's try to see him.

Has it been a while since you have seen him? If your prayers seem stale, it probably has. If your faith seems to be trembling, perhaps your vision of him has blurred. If you can't find power to face your problems, perhaps it is time to face him.

One warning. Something happens to a person who has witnessed his Majesty. He becomes addicted. One glimpse of the King and you are consumed by a desire to see more of him and say more about him. Pew-warming is no longer an option. Junk religion will no longer suffice. Sensation-seeking is needless. Once you have seen his face you will forever long to see it again.

(From *God Came Near* by Max Lucado)

RESPONSE

Use these questions to share more deeply with each other.

7. In what way can meeting Jesus change a person's life?

_____

_____

_____

8. Describe your first encounter with Jesus.

_____

_____

_____

9. In what way has your relationship with Jesus Christ grown and matured?

_____

_____

_____

PRAYER

Father, thank you for sending your Son to free us from the penalty of sin. And thank you for giving us your Holy Spirit to help us recognize and accept Jesus as our Savior. Guide us into a deeper relationship with you, so that when we go through difficult times, we can run to you and rest secure in your presence.

JOURNALING

Take a few moments to record your personal insights from this lesson.

How has meeting Jesus impacted my life?

ADDITIONAL QUESTIONS

10. In what way can life's problems and disappointments interfere with our communion with God?

_____

_____

_____

11. What can believers do when God seems far away?

_____

_____

_____

12. What steps can you take to nurture your relationship with Jesus?

_____

_____

_____

For more Bible passages on knowing Jesus, see John 10:14–27; Ephesians 1:15–17; Philippians 3:8–10; 2 Timothy 1:12; 1 John 2:3–6,29; 3:1–3; 4:13–16.

To complete the Book of Luke during this twelve-part study, read Luke 24:1–53.

ADDITIONAL THOUGHTS

ADDITIONAL THOUGHTS

LEADERS' NOTES

LESSON ONE

Question 5: More often than not, when faced with a situation that requires great faith, we respond with doubt instead. We naturally question what we can't immediately prove. Discuss with group members how they might have responded had they been in Zechariah's shoes.

Question 11: No matter how much we doubt it, our God is capable of doing incredible things! You may want to open this discussion with Ephesians 3:20–21 which says, "With God's power working in us, God can do much, much more than anything we can ask or imagine. To him be glory in the church and in Christ Jesus for all time, forever and ever. Amen."

LESSON TWO

Question 6: While Jesus had compassion for the physical suffering of people, his greatest concern was the state of their hearts. In Mark 1:38, Jesus says that the reason he has come is to preach, and in Luke 19:10 he says he has come to seek and save the lost. He knew that what was on the outside was only temporary, but what was on the inside would last forever. Do we have this same perspective in our interaction with people? What do we tend to focus on?

Question 8: You may also want to encourage group members to think about how they might grow in this area. In what ways should their faith affect others, but doesn't? And what can they do about this?

LESSON THREE

Question 2: Again, we see that Jesus was concerned with the heart. While the Pharisees focused on the externals—the outward conformity to the letter of the law, Jesus focused on the internal heart of the law. Therefore, he was more concerned with doing good and restoring a life than conforming to the mandates of the Pharisees.

Question 9: So often, the more pressure we're facing, the more we feel that we don't have time to pray. We couldn't be more wrong! Just look at Jesus' example. He dealt with more stress than most of us will ever encounter. And even though he was God, albeit in the form of a man, he still found it so necessary to pray that he made the time to do so, even if it meant he had to get up early or stay up all night. Shouldn't we learn from him?

LESSON FOUR

Question 4: To a Jew, the carrying on of the family line was extremely important. Sons were considered the ultimate blessing from God. For this mother to be left without her husband and without any sons would have made her pain and grief at this funeral all the more intense.

Question 12: You may want to give the group a little time to set some goals in this area. Have them think through specific, practical ways they could show compassion to that person. Ask group members to share, then spend some time praying for each other and the individuals mentioned. The next time you meet, you may want to ask group members how they did at putting the truths they learned into practice.

LESSON FIVE

Question 4: Give the group a moment to evaluate themselves in light of this parable. Consider these questions: Which of the four soils is most representative of your life? If you're not like the good ground, and you want to change, what can you do?

Question 12: Hebrews 4:12 and 2 Timothy 3:16–17 both speak of the power of God's Word to change our lives. Have the group take a look at these verses and talk about how they have seen these truths worked out in their own lives.

LESSON SIX

Question 1: You may also want to have group members compare and contrast this with how they would answer the question themselves.

Question 9: Consider having the group look at Paul's words in Galatians 2:20, "I was put to death on the cross with Christ, and I do not live anymore—it is Christ who lives in me. I still live in my body, but I live by faith in the Son of God who loved me and gave his life to save me." Ask additional questions, such as, How does this compare with what you have read in Luke? And, practically, what should this look like in your life on a daily basis?

Question 11: Ask group members to identify why it's difficult for them to share in those circumstances. Is it pride? Fear of being rejected? Do they not know how to express their views? Sometimes, if we can figure out *why* we find something difficult, we can get to work on doing something about it.

LESSON SEVEN

Question 8: In Matthew's account of the Lord's Prayer, he prefaces the prayer with some words from Jesus on this very issue. It may be helpful to have the group look at Matthew 6:7–8 before answering the question.

Question 9: Some suggestions include writing down your prayers, praying out loud, and "praying back" Bible verses as prayers to God. Also, try not to use "Christian lingo" in your prayers, and don't use big words unless you're sure you really know what they mean. It may help to try to pray with the simple words of a child.

LESSON EIGHT

Question 9: We find one good step in Philippians 4:6, where it says, "Do not worry about anything, but pray and ask God for everything you need, always giving thanks." Whenever we're tempted to worry, we should pray! You may even want to ask group members to share something they're worried about and then spend some time praying together.

Question 10: It's clear from Proverbs that planning is different from worrying, and that it's good to plan ahead—as long as we recognize God's control over those plans and we entrust them to him. If you'd like to explore this further you can look at Proverbs 15:22, 16:1, 16:3, 16:9, 19:21, 20:18, and 21:5.

LESSON NINE

Question 6: In addition to what Luke teaches us, 1 John 1:9 tells us what God will do if we confess our sins. It says, "If we confess our sins, he will forgive our sins, because we can trust God to do what is right. He will cleanse us from all the wrongs we have done."

Question 10: If your group is interested in further exploring the issue of favoritism, you can have them read James 2:1–13.

LESSON TEN

Question 3: For more on Jesus' heart for Jerusalem take a look at Matthew 23:37. You may want to open your discussion with these words of Jesus.

Question 7: Consider having group members justify their answers to the question. What do they base their definition of worship on? For example, do they base it on tradition and the things "they grew up with," or on how it makes them feel? What biblical principles is their definition based on?

LESSON ELEVEN

Question 2: Romans 6:23 tells us that the wages of our sin is death. Someone had to make that payment, and Jesus made it on our behalf. First Peter 3:18 says that Christ himself suffered for sins once. He was not guilty, but he suffered for those who are guilty to bring you to God. For more on this, you can read 2 Corinthians 5:17–21 and Hebrews 9:22–28 (especially verses 22 and 28).

Question 10: Take a look at 1 Corinthians 15:12–19. This is one place where Scripture tells us how our lives would be different without the resurrection. Paul writes that if Christ has not been raised, then your faith has nothing to it. We are still guilty. We should praise God that Jesus did indeed die and rise again!

LESSON TWELVE

Question 6: Jesus discusses the role of the Holy Spirit in John 14:15–17, 25–26 and 15:26.

Question 9: If anyone in your group is having a hard time identifying growth in their relationship with Jesus, you may want to spend some talking with them individually at another time. See if you can find out if that person is truly saved and just not growing, or if perhaps they have never truly entered into a relationship with Jesus.

ADDITIONAL NOTES

ADDITIONAL NOTES

ADDITIONAL NOTES

ADDITIONAL NOTES

ACKNOWLEDGMENTS

Keller, Philip. *A Gardener Looks at the Fruits of the Spirit*, copyright 1986, Word, Inc., Dallas, Texas.

Lucado, Max. *And the Angels Were Silent*, Questar Publishers, Multnomah Books, copyright 1992 by Max Lucado.

Lucado, Max. *God Came Near*, Questar Publishers, Multnomah Books, copyright 1987 by Max Lucado.

Lucado, Max. *He Still Moves Stones,* copyright 1993, Word Inc., Dallas, Texas.

Lucado, Max. *In the Eye of the Storm,* copyright 1991, Word Inc., Dallas, Texas.

Lucado, Max. *On the Anvil*, copyright 1985 by Max Lucado. Used by permission of Tyndale House Publishers, Inc. All rights reserved.

Lucado, Max. *Six Hours One Friday*, Questar Publishers, Multnomah Books, copyright 1989 by Max Lucado.